Chloé Perarnau

THE WALKABOUT ORCHESTRA

Postcards from around the world

WIDE EYED EDITIONS

VIOLINS

CELLO

VIOLA

DOUBLE BASS

FLUTE

PIANO

 HARP

 CYMBALS

 TRIANGLE

 SAXOPHONE

 TRUMPET

 TROMBONE

 BASS DRUM

TUBA

 OBOE

 CLARINET

 BASSOON

ICELAND

DEAR MAESTRO,

I AM IN ICELAND, IN A LITTLE FISHING VILLAGE!
THE VOLCANO SEEMS TO LIKE IT WHEN I PLAY THE
BIG BASS DRUM, AS THE MUSIC ROCKS IT TO SLEEP.
THE LOCAL PEOPLE ARE QUITE HAPPY THAT IT IS
SLEEPING SOUNDLY. SINCE I'VE BEEN HERE, I HAVE
REPAINTED THE HOUSE AND PREPARED SMOKED FISH
FOR THE WINTER.   BEST WISHES, MICHEL
                                        PERCUSSION

U.S.A.

Dear Maestro,

We have arrived in New Orleans, in time for Mardi Gras! People in disguises fill the streets. There are feathers, beads, floats and music all over the French Quarter. Thomas tries to make his double bass heard, Dolores sits on the edge of the Mississippi with her cello, and I think I have found the best float so far!

François, Thomas, and Dolores
Viola, double bass, cello

THOSE MARDI GRAS CAKES LOOK DELICIOUS ...
Walker's
MARDI GRAS
INDEED, BUT IT'S NOT GOING TO HELP US FIND OUR STRING PLAYERS!
WHAT A JOYFUL PARTY, MAESTRO!

ANSWERS

DID YOU FIND EVERYONE?
THE MUSICIANS ARE MARKED WITH RED CIRCLES.
THE BLACK CIRCLES SHOW THE THINGS THE YELLOW BIRD IS LOOKING FOR.

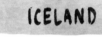

For my nieces and nephews, Lola, Zélie,
Arwen, Solal and Timéo. – C.P.

Brimming with creative inspiration, how-to projects, and useful information to enrich your everyday life, Quarto Knows is a favorite destination for those pursuing their interests and passions. Visit our site and dig deeper with our books into your area of interest: Quarto Creates, Quarto Cooks, Quarto Homes, Quarto Lives, Quarto Drives, Quarto Explores, Quarto Gifts, or Quarto Kids.

First published in the U.K. and the U.S.A. in 2018 by Wide Eyed Editions,
an imprint of The Quarto Group, 142 W 36th Street, 4th Floor, New York, NY 10018, U.S.A.
T (612) 344-8100 F (612) 344-8692 **www.QuartoKnows.com**

First published in France in 2016 under the title *L'Orchestre* by L'Agrume,
102, rue Saint-Maur, 75011, Paris, France
www.lagrume.org

Copyright © Editions L'Agrume 2016
Translation copyright © Wide Eyed Editions 2018
This edition was published by arrangement with The Picture Book Agency, France

ISBN 978-1-78603-079-5

Illustrated with ink and retouched digitally
This book has been handlettered

Translated by Marie Bédrune
Designed by Karissa Santos
Edited by Katy Flint
Published by Rachel Williams and Jenny Broom
Production by Jenny Cundill

Manufactured in Dongguan, China [TL] 122017

9 8 7 6 5 4 3 2 1